MORRIS M

Ray Newell

SHIRE PUBLICATIONS

Published in Great Britain in 2011 by Shire Publications
Ltd, Midland House, West Way, Botley, Oxford OX2 0PH,
United Kingdom.
44-02 23rd Street, Suite 219, Long Island City,
NY 11101, USA.

E-mail: shire@shirebooks.co.uk   www.shirebooks.co.uk

© 2009 Ray Newell. First published 2009; reprinted 2010
and 2011.

Every attempt has been made by the Publishers to secure
the appropriate permissions for materials reproduced in
this book. If there has been any oversight we will be happy
to rectify the situation and a written submission should be
made to the Publishers.

A CIP catalogue record for this book is available from the
British Library.

Shire Library no. 277   •   ISBN-13: 978 0 74780 762 9

Ray Newell has asserted his right under the Copyright,
Designs and Patents Act, 1988, to be identified as the
author of this book.

Designed by Ken Vail Graphic Design, Cambridge, UK and
typeset in Perpetua and Gill Sans.
Printed in China through Worldprint Ltd.

11 12 13 14 15   12 11 10 9 8 7 6 5 4 3

COVER IMAGE
A delightful artistic representation, dating from the
mid 1950s, showing the clean-cut lines of the
Morris Minor Series II four-door saloon

TITLE PAGE IMAGE
'A small car with big car features' was a recurring
theme used to good effect by the publicity department
at Morris Motors Ltd. Artistic licence is clearly evident
in this advert.

CONTENTS PAGE IMAGE
The success of the Morris Minor was heralded at every
opportunity to increase sales further, as in this early
brochure for the 1,098cc Morris 1000 models.

ACKNOWLEDGEMENTS
The author wishes to acknowledge the help, support and
encouragement offered by Nick Wright and Russell
Butcher in the planning and production of this publication.

Photographs and illustrations are acknowledged as follows
with grateful thanks: British Motor Industry Heritage
Trust, pages 8, 9 (top and middle), and 49;
National Motor Museum, pages 9 (bottom), and 60;
John Podpadec, page 10; John Colley, pages 22, 33, 34
(middle and bottom), 48, 54, 56, 61 (bottom) and 62;
Fraser McAskill, page 23; Oxford Mail, page 24; Robin
Beardmore, page 34 (top); Richard Cownden, page 37;
Simon Marsboll, page 55; Roger Tennyson, page 58
(bottom); John Ford, page 59. The remaining photographs
and illustrations are from the author's collection.

CONTENTS

THE EARLY YEARS

Above: The first
Morris car,
produced in 1912.

THE TRADITION of Morris vehicles dates back to the beginning of the twentieth century, when a young entrepreneur, William Richard Morris, developed his interest in motorcycles into a thriving sales and repair business in High Street, Oxford. Within a decade, purpose-built premises, named the Morris Garage, had been established in Longwall Street, Oxford, and by 1913 Morris's long-held ambition to design and build his own car had been achieved. The car,

Right:
Lord Nuffield
(William Richard
Morris) pictured
in the garden of
his home, Nuffield
Place, in
Oxfordshire. From
humble beginnings
as a cycle repairer,
he became
Britain's leading
motor-vehicle
manufacturer
and head
of the Nuffield
Organisation.

the Bullnose Oxford, was the forerunner to many other famous models, including the Morris Cowley of 1915, the Morris Minor of 1928, the Morris Isis of 1930, the Morris Ten of 1933 and the Morris Eight of 1934.

The success of the Morris range was based on a hard-earned reputation for 'quality' motor cars, and it brought financial security and public recognition for William Morris, who became a baronet in 1929, Baron Nuffield in 1934, and Viscount Nuffield in 1938. In the best tradition of business enterprise, Morris's company grew from its tentative beginnings in the cycle repair trade, with a working capital of £4, into a multi-million-pound motor manufacturer. Lord Nuffield became well-known as a public benefactor, making generous donations estimated at £30 million to medical and educational causes. His reputation as a shrewd, if at times uncompromising, businessman was aptly demonstrated in 1921, when, in the midst of a sales slump following soaring price increases after the First World War, and faced with rising costs, he cut the price of all Morris models by £100. As a result sales rose, the company drew ahead of its rivals and many new enterprises were bought or started. Morris Motors Ltd expanded, Morris Commercials was established, the MG Car Company was formed, and the original concern of Morris Garages Ltd continued as a distribution centre. The Wolseley Company was acquired in 1927 and the Riley Company taken over in 1928. The manufacturing plants at Cowley and Abingdon, near Oxford, were expanded, and many supporting component factories were established, including radiators and bodies branches, and the purchase of the SU Carburettor Company. It was inevitable that they would eventually come together under one umbrella organisation; this happened in 1940 with the formation of the Nuffield Organisation.

Above:
The Nuffield
Organisation logo.

Below: The two-millionth Nuffield vehicle, a four-door Morris Minor produced in 1951 on Lord Nuffield's seventy-fourth birthday.

FROM CONCEPT TO REALITY: THE SERIES MM

IT WAS at this time, at the beginning of the Second World War, that attention focused on the need to produce a new small Morris car. Under the guidance of Miles Thomas, Vice Chairman and Managing Director of the Nuffield Organisation, and Vic Oak, Chief Engineer at Morris Motors Ltd, early plans were laid, and the expertise of Alec Issigonis, a young engineer who had joined the company in 1936 from Rootes, was sought. Issigonis was highly regarded by Oak, and a measure of this was the fact that the new small car project was entrusted to him. With two able assistants, Jack Daniels, an expert on chassis and suspension, and Reg Job, a former Pressed Steel employee with considerable experience in body design, Issigonis had the nucleus of a small but effective team. Wartime projects assumed great importance, and the team was forced to divide its efforts between development work on the new car and numerous military machines, including armoured cars, tanks and amphibious motor vehicles.

Spurred on by the enthusiasm of Alec Issigonis, and the prospect of a unique opportunity to design a new vehicle from start to finish, they made good progress. From the inspirational sketches provided by Issigonis, Daniels and Job set to work, first producing scale models of the proposed design, before progressing to the production of a fully working prototype vehicle in 1943. Codenamed EX/SX/86, the new model was known as the Mosquito. Miles Thomas almost certainly influenced the choice of name because of his interest in aviation and his experience as a First World War fighter pilot.

Issigonis and Daniels drew on their experience too. They had worked together on the first monocoque design for Morris Motors Ltd, the Morris M Ten, and their respective wartime projects also involved work on independent front suspension and torsion bars. They resolved to incorporate these features into the Mosquito, along with rack-and-pinion steering, and small 14-inch

An early picture of the prototype Mosquito, codenamed EX/SX/86, dating from 1943. Note the louvred bonnet, an aid to a unique cooling system that employed a radiator mounted to the rear of the engine block.

road wheels. All this, allied to striking styling lines, meant that they were already breaking new ground.

Seeking to have a hand in almost every aspect of the car, Issigonis turned his attention to the engine. He favoured the use of an experimental flat four water-cooled engine, which utilised a three-speed gearbox with column gearchange. 800cc and 1,100cc versions were later used in the Mosquito and in subsequent prototypes. Despite numerous teething problems, both Issigonis and Daniels would have persevered with the flat four engine and would have preferred to see it used in production cars. That it did not happen was, as Daniels recalled, due to 'inter-factory politics'. The cost of developing a new engine for full-scale production was deemed too great, and for practical as well as economic reasons the engine used in the Morris Eight came back into the reckoning. With some slight modifications, this side-valve engine became the favoured choice for the production models.

Issigonis favoured the use of a flat four engine in the new car, but failed to persuade the management to adopt it for production.

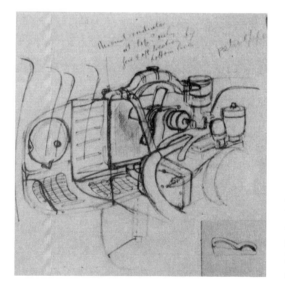

Refinements to the prototype cars continued until 1948. In all, eight prototypes were used. Because it was decided to adopt the 918cc side-valve engine with the corresponding gearbox, the bench-type front seat and column gearchange were dispensed with in favour of a floor change and two separate front seats. More significantly, there was a momentous eleventh-hour decision by Issigonis to change the dimensions of the car. All the prototypes were 57 inches

A styling mock-up dating from 1945, showing that the front end and headlamp arrangement was still under consideration.

Early in the planning it was decided that the new small vehicle would be available as saloon and tourer models. This narrow-bodied prototype Tourer dates from 1947.

This 1948 pre-production model closely resembles the final styling of the new car. Significantly, it has the wider body with the corresponding 4-inch strip in the bonnet, a split bumper with a concealed fillet, and an unusual badge arrangement.

Jack Daniels and Reg Job with the first Morris Minor off the production line, and one of the earliest models of the prototype Mosquito.

wide, the same width as the Morris Eight. Issigonis felt that this was too narrow, and so he ordered that one of the prototypes be sawn in half lengthways and the two halves moved apart. At 4 inches apart, Issigonis was satisfied. Reg Job then had to accommodate this extra width: it required the checking and rechecking of many hundreds of dimensions.

The change had serious implications for the whole design of the car. Apart from the gain in internal dimensions, the main benefit was increased stability and improved road-holding. The body panels had to be modified, and the most obvious change was the insertion of an extra 4-inch flat strip in the bonnet – a feature of all subsequent models. There was also the need to add an extra 4 inches to the bumpers. As they had already gone into production on a large scale, they were cut in half and an extra fillet was added to join them together.

With these changes and – at Lord Nuffield's insistence – under the name of Morris Minor rather than Mosquito, the first production model, a two-door saloon, was made on 20 September 1948.

From the outset the Morris Minor was heralded as a world-beater – hence the multilingual approach adopted on this early brochure.

Below and below right: Early brochure art.

The first post-war Motor Show was held at Earls Court in London in October 1948. Three new Morris models were on display: the Morris Six MS, the Morris Oxford MO and the Morris Minor Series MM. Two-door saloon and tourer versions of the Morris Minor were on show and, much against earlier expectations, it was these models that attracted most attention.

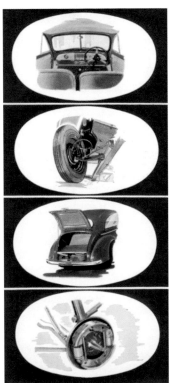

Supreme in Economy

The new **MORRIS MINOR** makes the most of your petrol, goes farther on a tankful. Traditional Morris reliability and low maintenance are inherent in this modern design.

The all-new Morris Minor was the undoubted star of the 1948 Motor Show held in London.

The motoring press was full of praise for the car billed as 'the world's supreme small car'. *Autocar* magazine described it as 'beyond expectations'. The *Motor* claimed 'it was a car which pleased drivers and passengers alike' and, in a glowing tribute to its designer, went on to say that the car 'approached perfection'.

Road testers also expressed their approval and complimented the road-holding characteristics of the new car, its comfort, tasteful interior design, and economical use of fuel. At £358 10s 7d it was competitively priced and, not surprisingly, demand outstripped supply.

The weak economy of post-war Britain made it essential for exports to take priority over the home market. Over 75 per cent of all Series MM cars produced were exported. Furthermore, there were restrictions in Britain on the purchase of new cars, so acquiring one of the highly rated Morris Minors was regarded as a major achievement. With the car's popularity undiminished, additional assembly tracks were laid at Cowley and production was stepped up.

Because of its superlative springing, the MORRIS MINOR is easy on tyres. Accessibility of components is a big feature. This is a real motorcar scaled down. Wider-than-ever seating, controlled ventilation, independent front suspension by torsion bars, and new, strong "Mono-construction" for extra strength and safety make the MORRIS MINOR the supreme small family car.

Left: The striking lines of the Series MM Tourer with the side screens detached. The majority of early cars went for export, so this model is comparatively rare in the United Kingdom.

Below: The labour-intensive production lines at Cowley. Such was the demand for the car that new assembly lines had to be installed.

To take full advantage of the phenomenal power output of the MORRIS MINOR husky engine, an easy-shift, four-speed synchromesh transmission is provided.

Seven cubic feet of space for luggage makes it easy to take the family on holiday. Access is by hinged rear trunk lid or from interior. Spare wheel always accessible in separate locker.

Access to the wide rear seats is easy by tipping the front seats forward. Rear passengers have full-width seats, plenty of room for long legs, and good head-room.

Below: American lighting regulations forced a change in the headlamp arrangement, much to the annoyance of Alec Issigonis.

Within months of the start of production, Issigonis and his team had to go back to the drawing board. Impending legislation in the United States laid down new regulations governing the height of headlamps: this meant that the grille-mounted headlamps of the newly announced Series MM would have to go. Much to Issigonis's annoyance, the front-end styling had to be modified in order to accommodate the headlamps in the wings. Reg Job, commenting on subsequent attempts to update the shape of the Minor, claimed that the raising of the headlamps and the resultant change to the front wings was 'all we got away with'.

Supreme in Comfort

Enjoy the new *Lull-abye Ride* in the **MORRIS**! Wider-than-ever seating, deep-sprung for lasting ease (with all seats within the wheelbase) and controlled ventilation.

NO PRICE PENALTY ON CONVERTIBLES! You pay the same low price as for the two-door sedan—actually hundreds of dollars under other makes.

When the bonnet is raised, refilling with oil and water can be accomplished easily. Phenomenal accessibility reduces maintenance costs.

You don't often have to change a wheel on the road these days, but when you do, Morris make it easy by means of the high-lift jack provided.

The problem of parking disappears almost entirely with this handy, easy-to-park Morris Minor. Light medium-ratio steering makes it a car for the ladies, too.

Although the change was effected as early as December 1948 on a prototype American model, it was not implemented for the whole range until September 1950, when the new four-door saloon was introduced. In keeping with the trend, this model was available for export only when launched. The only other significant changes to the Series MM were the return to a single-piece bumper and valance with the advent of the new-style wings, the additional option of a heater when the engine block was modified to take a water pump, and the changes from detachable celluloid side screens on the tourer models to fixed glass side windows. With this change the tourer was redesignated 'Convertible'.

The welcome expansion of the model range, and the subtle updating of the specifications boosted sales, and led to greater optimism that potential buyers in Britain would get a larger market share. Tremendous efforts were made to expand and reinvigorate the worldwide dealer network, and much was made of the parts and servicing facilities available to maintain the cars both at home and abroad.

Above: The Series MM models had many innovative features: torsion bar suspension; excellent load space; illuminated engine bay; easy jacking; safe, sure braking; and monocoque construction.

The NEW

PUBLICATION No. NEL.165

FOUR DOOR MORRIS MINOR

The model range was expanded in 1950 with the introduction of the four-door saloon.

15

The initial euphoria surrounding the Morris Minor proved to be justified and the expectations expressed regarding economy, durability and practicality were, if anything, exceeded. The vehicles were promoted in the media across the world in many different ways, including epic long-distance journeys, annual motor shows, and motor sport. There was even an entry in the 1949 Monte Carlo Rally, resulting in a second-place finish in the Coup des Dames. Soon attention was being given to improvements in overall performance. Companies such as the Alta Car and Engineering Company and Derrington Ltd offered engine conversions that substantially increased acceleration, and raised the top speed from 62 mph to 75 mph. Monaro Motors Ltd in Australia offered a similar conversion that proved popular, as did the conversion from Mazengarb side valve to overhead valve.

Above: The spacious interior of the four-door saloon.

Below: Initially the new four-door saloon was available for export only.

After-sale accessories for the Morris Minor were widely advertised, though some were very much niche market products. For instance, a tourer-to-coupé conversion was offered by Jarvis & Sons, and Airstream offered the opportunity to increase the value of the convertible by converting it to a saloon by having an aluminium hard top fitted.

It was boom time for the Morris Minor, a fact endorsed by total sales of 176,002 by the time production of the Series MM finished in February 1953.

Above: North America was one of the leading export markets in the early 1950s. The saloon models were marketed as sedans.

Left: The 'Tourer' designation for open-topped models was changed to 'Convertible' when fixed rear windows replaced the detachable side screens used on early models.

MORRIS *Minor* 4-DOOR SALOON

" Quality First" all the way through

MORRIS *Minor* 2-DOOR SALOON

"Quality First"— all the way through

MORRIS *Minor* CONVERTIBLE

" Quality First"—all the way through

TO ONE MILLION AND BEYOND

IN FEBRUARY 1952 the Nuffield Organisation merged with the Austin Motor Company to form the British Motor Corporation (BMC). Given the intense rivalry that existed between Lord Nuffield and Herbert Austin, it seemed an unlikely alliance. However, once established, it made BMC one of the largest motor-manufacturing concerns in Europe.

An immediate consequence for the Morris Minor was the decision to replace the side-valve engine with the more up-to-date 803cc overhead-valve engine, which had already been fitted to Austin's rival small car, the Austin A30. The change offered improved performance in terms of increased acceleration, with a 0–30 mph time of 8.4 seconds and a 0–50 mph time of 25.7 seconds, an improvement of nearly 13 seconds.

While this aspect of the car's performance was to be welcomed, there were reservations about the effectiveness of the gearbox. The *Autocar*, in its review of the new Series II saloon, lamented the demise of the side-valve close-ratio Morris gearbox, because the new Austin box had less effective synchromesh and gave maximum speeds in second and third gear of only 28 mph and 42 mph respectively. In their view, 'the low third gear showed up the modest power output of the engine'.

The only outward sign of the advent of the new Series II Morris Minor models was a change to the bonnet badge and the adoption of an 'M' motif.

Two-door and four-door saloons, along with the popular convertibles, remained in production, and in October 1953 they were joined by a new model, the Series II Traveller's Car. Unlike the Series II light commercial vehicles, which were first introduced in May 1953 and had a separate chassis, the Traveller was made of the same unitary construction as the saloons and convertibles. The ash-wood frame, bolted to the steel floor pan, supported an aluminium roof panel that was bolted to the front cab. The side panels were also made of aluminium, but the rear wings were made of steel. In overall length the Traveller was 1 inch longer than the saloon. The rear seat folded down to provide a large loading platform, making it an attractive vehicle for businessmen, commercial travellers and families.

Opposite:
'Quality first' was the watchword for Morris Motors Ltd. No chance was missed to promote the success of the company and its manufacturing record, which was second to none among European car producers.

Right: The Austin-
derived 803cc
A Series engine was
the first tangible
sign of co-operation
between Austin and
Morris following the
merger to form
BMC in 1952.

Below: The Morris
Minor was a
quintessentially
British car. The
distinctive features
of the Morris Minor
Series II four-door
saloon are shown
to good effect in
a delightful period
setting.

Left: The Morris Minor Series II Traveller model was a belated addition to the range in October 1953, and proved an immediate success.

Below: Every opportunity was taken to market the new models. Here a unique cut-away model, exhibited at a European motor show, shows the salient features of the mechanical components, including the 803cc engine.

In 1954 the Morris Minor range underwent a major facelift. The honeycomb grille, so long a feature of the car, was replaced by a slatted grille. This necessitated repositioning the sidelights, which now moved to the wing. The rear lamps were redesigned and enlarged to accommodate a bigger

Right: The 1954 makeover saw the introduction of a slatted front grille and revised frontal arrangement, though the split windscreen remained. The new look was heavily promoted in contemporary advertising literature.

Below:
The convertible models grew in popularity and increasing numbers were made available for customers in the United Kingdom.

reflector. Inside, a new fascia was installed. This featured a centrally positioned speedometer with open glove boxes on either side.

THE MORRIS MINOR 1000

Further developments followed in 1956. The character of the Morris Minor was changed when the split windscreen was dispensed with and a single-piece curved screen was fitted. The rear screen was enlarged too and, as a consequence of these changes, the whole of the roof pressing had to be altered. All-round visibility was improved immensely and, with a newly

MORRIS MINOR
Facts for Salesmen

YOUR "WALK AROUND" SALES GUIDE

Your " walk around " sales guide. Starting from the left-hand-side front door handle, we walk round the car in a clockwise direction, pointing out the features as we go.

▶ MAIN SELLING POINTS

1. "Mono - construction." Most modern method of car construction—is stronger, safer, lighter, lasts longer.

2. "Quality First" finish inside and out—degree of finish is remarkably high for price. Six coats of paint, whole body completely rustproofed.

3. Choice of three models—2-door saloon, 4-door saloon, convertible (lowest priced).

4. Modern, pleasing appearance—no awkward curves not ultra-streamlined. Is a small car with big-car lines.

5. All seats are within the

Publication No. H.5330

Nothing was left to chance to boost sales. Salesmen had a comprehensive guide that ensured that all positive aspects of the cars could be highlighted to prospective customers.

The introduction of the 948cc Morris Minor 1000 in 1956 represented the most substantial change to the specification since the Minor's introduction in 1948.

uprated engine and gearbox, the Morris Minor 1000, as it is now known, received a new lease of life.

Engine size was increased to 948cc. The power output increased by 20 per cent from 30 to 37 brake horsepower and the top speed from 61 to 73 mph. 0–30 mph now took only 6.8 seconds, and 0–60 mph was recorded as 30 seconds. The gearbox, with a remote-control gearshift, was a great improvement on the previous 803cc box, and the improved gear ratios allowed for 35 mph in second gear and 60.5 mph in third.

The verdict of contemporary road testers was that the Minor was still 'full of appeal, ahead of its rivals' and that it 'provided for the family man comfort, flexibility and good economy'. Furthermore, 'by using the power and road holding provided, sports car cornering and acceleration were possible'.

The new models proved popular and, though the main mechanical and body-styling specifications remained virtually unchanged between 1956 and 1962, the internal appointments changed significantly. Three revisions of the interior trim took place, with the introduction of leather-faced seating and the use of two-tone upholstery being the most noticeable. Variations also occurred in the use of glove-box lids, which at different times seemed to

Contemporary advertising brochures emphasised the universal appeal of the Morris Minor, the emergence of an increasing number of female drivers, and the suitability of the Minor for family use.

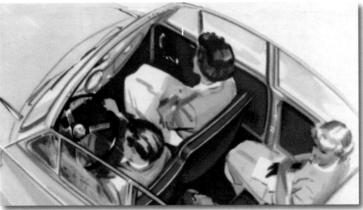

Room for all the family.

Below: Improved all-round visibility was a big feature of the Morris Minor 1000.

come into and go out of favour. The extensive choice of complementary trim and paint combinations available continued to add freshness to the model range. One such was Highway Yellow, complemented with blue upholstery, trim and carpets; this certainly stood out and, perhaps unsurprisingly, fewer than seven hundred vehicles were finished to this specification.

Nevertheless, with these improvements, sales continued to increase, and the Nuffield export division continued to flourish. The Morris Minor was popular in

Britain and elsewhere. The hopes of the original design team and the expectations of the management at Morris Motors that there would be potential for 250,000 units in the short term had been greatly exceeded, and the sales were showing no signs of diminishing.

By December 1960 it was estimated that total sales of all Morris Minor variants were approaching one million. It was decided that in order to mark this significant historical fact a special-edition Morris Minor would be produced. The car, appropriately dubbed the Minor Million, was painted in a delicate shade of lilac and had 'white gold' leather seats, with contrasting black piping. Commemorative 'Minor 1000000' badges were fitted to the bonnet and boot lid, and special wheel-rim embellishers were added. In all other respects the car was a standard 948cc two-door Morris Minor. 349 replicas of the 'Million' were produced and, as part of a publicity exercise to mark the fact that the Morris Minor was the first British vehicle to reach one million units in production, they were sent to distributors in the United Kingdom, Europe, Canada, the United States

History was made when sales of the Morris Minor reached one million. The distinctively coloured limited-edition model launched to mark the occasion was used for publicity in Britain and overseas. This Canadian celebration was typical.

and Australia. Information was strictly embargoed until 4 January 1961 but following this date there was an extensive flurry of publicity.

These cars are the only special-edition Morris Minors and, in spite of their colour, they are sought after as collectors' items. Over forty are known to have survived. At the same time BMC attempted to locate the oldest surviving Morris Minor production model. Provided that it had covered at least 100,000 miles, the owner was promised a new car in exchange for his old one. It was in this way that the first Morris Minor, NWL 576, was discovered. It was in quite a dilapidated state. However, following an extensive restoration, undertaken by BMC apprentices, it was put on public display. It still exists, and is one of the many exhibits at the British Heritage Motor Museum at Gaydon, Warwickshire. The new car offered in exchange was one of the limited edition Minor Millions, and was presented in a blaze of publicity to Cyril Swift in his home town of Sheffield.

Special features of the limited-edition model included 'Minor 1000000' badging.

Production continued past the one million mark, and in 1962 the Morris Minor received another major revamp. This time the engine size was boosted to 1,098cc. Power output increased to 48 brake horsepower, but a change of axle ratio from 4.55 to 4.22 meant that the top speed did not increase beyond the previous 73 mph. Acceleration was further improved with the 0–60 mph time being bettered by 6 seconds. Other improvements included a larger-diameter clutch, baulk ring synchromesh, larger front brakes, and a fresh air heater.

The last batch of improvements came in 1964. Most importantly, the seating was improved both in appearance and in comfort. Heat-formed vinyl seat covers and door panels in a range of complementary colours were fitted to saloon, convertible and Traveller models. A new-style fascia with a revised centrally placed speedometer that incorporated all warning lights was adopted. This was flanked by a lidded glove box on the passenger side, and an open glove box behind a new-style black two-spoked safety steering wheel. A combined key-operated ignition and starter switch was also adopted.

By 1966, when sealed-beam headlamp units were fitted, export sales had begun to decline. There was, however, still a thriving market in Britain as the Morris Minor retained its popularity. Despite competition from newer models such as the Mini and the Morris and Austin 1100/1300, sales of the Morris Minor remained strong enough for it to remain in production. The popular light commercial and Traveller models still commanded a significant market share.

20% more profitable power

BIG POWER STEP-UP *means-*

- Faster deliveries and wider operating range
- Longer, trouble-free life
- Greater value than ever

With its new 950 c.c. O.H.V. engine, the Morris ¼ Ton Van becomes more than ever 'the world's biggest small van buy!' The extra power means extra profits every way: by extending your delivery range; by carrying heavier loads faster, more easily; by ensuring a longer operational van-life.

And remember: this cost-cutting vehicle with a pint-size upkeep budget provides really big goods capacity—70 cu. ft.!

TWELVE MONTHS' WARRANTY

'QUALITY FIRST'

MORRIS

¼ TON VAN AND PICK-UP

SEE THE WORLD'S BIGGEST SMALL VAN BUY AT

THE LIGHT COMMERCIAL VEHICLES

LIGHT COMMERCIAL VEHICLES did not feature in the original line-up of post-war Morris Minor models when they went on public display for the first time at the Earls Court Motor Show in 1948. It was not until 1953, under the aegis of the newly formed British Motor Corporation (BMC), that the Morris Minor Quarter Ton van and pick-up models were announced, and the process of phasing out their predecessors, the Morris Eight-based 5 cwt vans (Z Series), began. Though designated the O Type Quarter Ton van and pick-up, the new models shared much of the front-end styling and almost all of the mechanical specifications of the already established Series II saloon and convertible models. For this reason, these early commercial vehicles are more commonly referred to as Series II vans and pick-ups.

Much was made of the compactness, versatility and economy of the new models, which were available in three options: complete van, complete pick-up with or without a canvas tilt, and a cab/chassis with the facility for coachbuilders to add custom-made bodies. Powered by the already well-established A Series 803cc overhead-valve engine, and constructed utilising an all-steel box-sectioned full-length chassis, the commercials had much to commend them and they sold well.

Boosted by pre-production orders from the Post Office for specially designed Post Office vans and telephone engineers' vans, Series II light commercial vehicle (LCV) sales flourished, and in three years exceeded 48,000. During this time, the LCVs had, like the rest of the range, undergone some restyling. In October 1954 a new-style fascia with a centrally mounted speedometer and a redesigned front grille with horizontal grille bars and repositioned sidelights were introduced. Two years later the Morris Minor 1000 range was announced and further changes were implemented. Morris 1000 LCVs adopted the one-piece windscreen, but much more important was the introduction of a much-needed uprated power unit. In terms of power and acceleration the 803cc engine and corresponding transmission had not been a resounding success, particularly so in the case of LCVs fitted with the low-compression version

29

The early versions of the Morris Minor Quarter Ton light commercials were promoted alongside the Morris Half Ton van and pick-up models that preceded them into production. Both utilised a separate chassis that allowed for custom-built bodies to be fitted.

of the engine. The introduction of a much livelier and smoother 948cc engine and gearbox was a welcome, if somewhat overdue, innovation. Morris 1000 LCV sales boomed. Over 100,000 948cc powered LCVs helped to boost overall sales to the record-breaking total of one million, which was reached in 1960.

Specialist conversion companies, some approved by the Nuffield Organisation, did thriving business in the 1950s, when it was popular to have side windows and rear seat conversions fitted to vans. This version was offered by Wadham Bros Ltd, based in Waterlooville, Hampshire.

MORRIS ¼-TON VAN AND PICK-UP

In late 1962 the engine size of the Morris Minor was increased still further. The model range was fitted with a 1,098cc overhead-valve engine, which further enhanced acceleration and performance. This, along with improved transmission, braking and interior styling refinements, revitalised interest in the vehicles.

Above: The flat-panelled sides of the LCVs proved ideal for promotional advertising, and provided welcome employment for traditional signwriters.

Left: Fleet users found the economy, reliability and versatility of the Morris Minor advantageous to their business. The RAC used the vans as service vehicles.

In the case of the LCV models, the increased power output allowed for a welcome increase in the payload capacity from 5 cwt to 6 cwt – so making them more attractive to potential customers. It signalled the end of the Quarter Ton Series commercials and prompted the advertising department to promote the new Morris 6 cwt Series III van as 'the world's biggest small van buy'.

In 1968 the payload was increased to 8 cwt and the rear springs were modified to take an extra leaf. The suspension was uprated to cope with the anticipated extra loading. 6 cwt versions remained in production alongside these new models. By this time BMC had been superseded by British Leyland, under the control of Lord Stokes, and Morris Minor vans and pick-ups were produced and marketed with Austin badging. Distinguishing features of these products of badge engineering were a crinkle-type slatted grille, Austin badging on the centre of the steering wheel and on the bonnet, and Austin hub caps.

Badge engineering was a popular phenomenon in the 1960s. In the case of the Morris Minor LCVs, Austin vans and pick-ups were marketed alongside the Morris models.

The last of the LCVs were produced in 1971 at Adderley Park, Birmingham, and although factory records were destroyed, it is estimated that a total of 326,626 Morris Minor light commercial vehicles were made. Of this total, some 50,000 were specially commissioned by the General Post Office to be used as mail vans and as telephone engineers' vans. With so many in service, Morris Minor Post Office vans became a familiar sight throughout

the British Isles and the Channel Islands. Many remained in service long after production ceased and at least one van was in use as late as 1982, albeit in the livery of British Telecom.

The special features of the GPO vehicles, which distinguish them from the rest of the LCVs made during a production run of nineteen years, are less familiar. The very early Post Office vehicles are scarce nowadays. They had the distinction of being equipped with rubber wings with headlamps fitted on top. There were few comforts for the postman in those days, with only one seat fitted and no heater – though there was the option of additional ventilation by means of an opening windscreen. Series III Post Office vehicles followed more conventional styling but are still easily identifiable with, among other features, a rather unusual security arrangement on the driver's door that used a Yale lock.

Apart from the GPO, many metropolitan and municipal authorities were fleet users of Morris Minor commercial vehicles. Service industries, wholesalers, retailers, farmers, builders and countless other tradesmen found the claims of the sales literature very persuasive. There was indeed a place for a Morris Minor commercial in any type of business. Grocers, newsagents, radio and television engineers, florists, seed merchants, wine and spirit merchants, dry cleaners, ironmongers, milliners and bakers were just a few of the widely differing trades that found that the Morris Minor commercials could provide a light, rapid delivery service at low cost.

Interior trim specifications differed on LCVs, with rubber mats, plain, flat-panelled seat covers and more durable painted millboard door cards.

During the years of production there was little else that could seriously rival the versatility and economy of these popular workhorses, a fact borne out by the GPO's long-standing contract. For the operator who preferred to have his own coachbuilt body fitted to his vehicles, the option of a cab/chassis was available. Gown vans, garage breakdown and recovery pick-ups, ice-cream vans and even specially adapted vans for Esso Blue and Aladdin Pink paraffin all used the Morris Minor chassis to good effect.

Not all the non-standard commercials were commissioned at the whim of individual owners. An extra-large van was manufactured in Denmark by the importing company DOMI. With a single rear door and extra length and height, its overall capacity was considerably increased. In spite of this and the innovative features, these models, which were produced in Series II and Series III specifications, remained a Danish option only. Elsewhere, unique limited production LCVs were produced. One of the most unusual was the double-cab Morris Minor pick-up assembled in Chile by Anglo-Chilean Autos Ltd.

The detailed specification of the Post Office telephone vans set them apart from all other Morris Minor LCVs: additional ventilation was provided by means of an opening windscreen; rubber wings with externally mounted headlamps were adopted in order to reduce repair costs from impact collisions that would have been incurred with traditional steel wings; specially designed trafficator boxes were used on vans so as to ensure adequate visibility from the rear.

The GPO Telephone Engineers' Vans were fitted out with specialised equipment.

The double cab was mounted on a standard chassis, featuring a much-reduced payload area. Remarkably, one example is known to have survived. While it is certainly a rare vehicle, it could be said to be the forerunner of the much bigger but hugely popular 4x4 double-cab pick-ups that have gained notoriety in the early twenty-first century.

Interest in the Morris Minor light commercial vehicles remains high and they are much sought

Many distinctive Morris Minor LCVs plied their trade, including those used by ice-cream companies, clothing retailers, high-street chain stores and individual entrepreneurs: pictured here are a high-topped delivery van used by Currys Ltd (left), and a high-topped gown van (below).

after today, both by enthusiasts wishing to restore them to original condition, and by modern businesses wanting an eyecatching vehicle to advertise their company. With new chassis and most body panels and mechanical parts available, owning and running a Morris Minor LCV is still a viable option in the twenty-first century. Alec Issigonis would have been proud of that.

NEW YORK — *Congratulations on a rave-able car*

KAMPALA — *Have awaited this car for years*

CAIRO — *Greatly impressed*

WELLINGTON — *New Morris Cars exceed all expectations*

MONTREAL — *It's a winner*

BARBADOS — *Beautiful and outstanding car*

SYDNEY — *Magnificent*

LISBON — *Heartiest congratulations*

GENEVA — *Great success assured*

AMERSFOORT — *Marvellous car*

NAIROBI — *Anticipate great future for this car*

TASMANIA — *Definitely surpasses any competitors*

CAPE TOWN — *A credit to the Nuffield organisation*

WORLD-WIDE PRAISE FOR THE MORRIS CARS

Morris Minor

Morris Oxford

Morris Six

MORRIS
The British Car with a World Appeal

EARLS COURT **Stand 167**

MORRIS MOTORS LIMITED, COWLEY, OXFORD. OVERSEAS BUSINESS: NUFFIELD EXPORTS LIMITED, OXFORD, AND 41 PICCADILLY, LONDON, W.1

PRODUCTION OVERSEAS

IN the motor-manufacturing industry 'CKD', which stands for 'completely knocked down', is the system by which vehicles are shipped abroad in component form, in easily transportable packing cases, ready for assembly in the market for which they are destined. This system of car assembly represented a major segment of Morris Minor production during, and indeed beyond, the period of twenty-two years when Morris Minors were in production in Britain.

The boom years were in the 1950s, when it was imperative, for both economic and social reasons, to rebuild and expand the British economy following the disruption of the war years. For many it was an austere time, with rationing still part of everyday life, but it was also a time of optimism, especially in the motor industry, where every company was seeking to expand its business. At Cowley in Oxford a new purpose-built factory was established to cope with the increasing demands of the export market for CKD models. Personnel were specially trained to assist with the establishment of overseas assembly plants, and in the Cowley works itself there was a demonstration bay where overseas personnel could study every aspect of assembly with standard Nuffield jigs and equipment, assisted by experienced assembly foremen and technologists.

In countries such as Australia, New Zealand, South Africa, India, Holland, Denmark, and the Republic of Ireland, special plants were opened and equipped to enable the assembly work to be undertaken to a consistent standard. Jigs, tools and fixtures were supplied, and special arrangements entered into for the supply of local materials for some components such as glass, batteries, tyres, upholstery and interior fitments. While the objective was to produce a vehicle to the same basic specification as the British-assembled product, the priority was to reduce costs and make use of local materials where possible. This obviously extended to the use of local labour.

The attractions of this method of production are substantial but the logistics of supplying all the necessary components were considerable, especially as there were 19,587 separate parts for one Morris Minor.

Opposite:
The worldwide appeal of the Morris Minor was reflected in opportunist promotional material that sought to enhance the reputation of Morris cars in general.

Above:
Exports were a high priority in post-war Britain. Transporters laden with Morris Minors bound for the ports were a common sight in the 1950s.

Opposite:
To cope with the huge expansion of the CKD operation for Nuffield exports, a new factory with 100,000 square feet of floor space was built at Cowley, Oxford.

Consequently the Nuffield operation had to be well organised. Packaging had to be as compact as possible to save on shipping costs, and delivery schedules had to be tightly observed to avoid contravening local tariff deadlines in various ports of entry. Success helped guarantee the advertising department's claim that the Morris Minor was indeed 'the world's supreme small car'.

In Ireland the cars were assembled by G. A. Brittain in Dublin. Records show that the first CKD Morris Minors despatched for export all went to Ireland. Eighteen Series MM saloons were sent in 1948, making Ireland the first overseas country to have Morris Minor production. G. A. Brittain assembled all versions of the Series MM, but after the introduction of the Series II models production was restricted to two-door and four-door saloons, with the occasional special-order convertible.

Brittain continued with production until 1971 and, like the Cowley factory, finished production by assembling a two-door saloon. The Irish-built cars had a number of unique features that distinguished them from their British counterparts. The grille panel and wheels were painted in the body colour, and the wing piping, which was normally matched to the body colour, was black on all models. The interior fittings differed too, with plain door

Specially trained operatives maximised the use of space when packing CKD components. Not a millimetre of space was wasted.

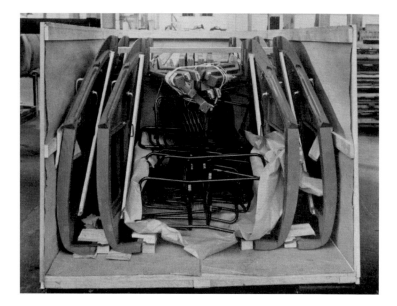

trims being used on late Morris 1000 models, rather than the heat-formed trim panels usually associated with Cowley-produced cars. Other distinguishing features include the sometimes unsightly welded bulkhead panel, which offers clear evidence of the CKD origins of the vehicles.

Another country that featured prominently in the production of Morris Minors was Holland. One saloon was assembled in 1949 in a factory owned by the Molenaar Company at Jutphaas, but production was stepped up after this, and in 1953 a much bigger factory was built at Amersfoort. However, only two-door and four-door saloon versions of the Series MM models were produced in Holland.

The Dutch company Molenaar was ideally suited to take on Morris Minor production. They had been producing MGs since 1932, and had added Morris models to their output in 1936. In addition they already had their own established suppliers of components, such as windows from Staalglas, tyres from Vredestein, lighting from Philips and paint from Valspar. The provision of such parts helped keep costs down at the point of entry into Holland. This was vital because in 1951 no car could be imported into Holland if it cost more than the Dutch equivalent of £420. The Dutch vehicles had left-hand drive and so there were some major differences from the British-made cars but, like the complete left-hand-drive cars exported to the United States, Dutch CKD models had the annoying feature of only one door lock (for all but the latest models). This component was supplied as for the right-hand-drive vehicles, so, to get

Left: In Ireland G.A. Brittain Ltd of Dublin built CKD saloon and convertible models. Trim and paint specifications differed. This 'new' unregistered vehicle survives in remarkable condition just as it left the factory.

Below: American advertising extolled the virtues of the Morris MINOR 1000 and priased its economical running costs.

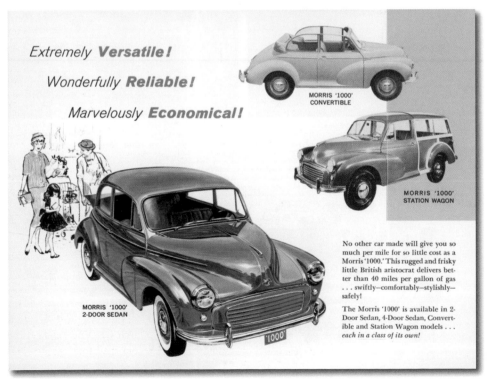

Extremely **Versatile!**

Wonderfully **Reliable!**

Marvelously **Economical!**

MORRIS '1000'
CONVERTIBLE

MORRIS '1000'
STATION WAGON

MORRIS '1000'
2-DOOR SEDAN

No other car made will give you so much per mile for so little cost as a Morris '1000.' This rugged and frisky little British aristocrat delivers better than 40 miles per gallon of gas ... swiftly—comfortably—stylishly—safely!

The Morris '1000' is available in 2-Door Sedan, 4-Door Sedan, Convertible and Station Wagon models ... *each in a class of its own!*

into the car, the driver had to first open the passenger door, unlock the driver's door from the inside and then walk around the car to get in. Production at the Amersfoort plant was successful and supported by a well-resourced dealer network. Volume sales continued until 1966, when the assembly of Morris Minors was ended.

The Dutch company Molenaar produced large numbers of CKD Morris Minors with a high local content. Locally sourced components included glass, tyres, paint and electrical parts.

It was about this time, too, that production ceased at the DOMI (Dansk Oversoisk Motor Industri) factory in Denmark. DOMI was a well-established company when Morris Minor assembly began, and was an obvious choice for CKD production. DOMI worked on the established principle of producing vehicles to meet local needs, and some of the Danish-built cars have unique features. With many of the vehicles being sold in Scandinavian countries such as Norway and Sweden, modifications were made to the engine ancillaries to facilitate easier starting in cold conditions. Like the Irish-built cars, later Danish-assembled Morris 1000 models had plain door panels. However, the most interesting omission from all post-1953 models is the famous bonnet motif, which was banned on the grounds of safety. Fortunately, the early-type bonnet flash used on Series MM and on Morris Minor light commercial vehicles was deemed to be an acceptable replacement.

Morris Minor production was not confined to European assembly plants. Such was the appeal of the Morris Minor, and the strength of the Nuffield Organisation's promotion and marketing campaigns, that plants in Australia, New Zealand, South Africa, and India all produced the Morris Minor in substantial numbers, particularly during the 1950s and 1960s.

Australia was the largest overseas market for the Morris Minor. Initially the cars were shipped as complete vehicles, and regular shipments from Britain were commonplace in the years immediately following the launch of the Morris Minor Series MM. However, the establishment of a large-scale production plant at Zetland, New South Wales, changed all that. Nuffield (Australia) Pty Ltd commenced assembly of CKD models with a high local

The DOMI assembly plant achieved some notoriety on account of the specially designed, extended DOMI van, featuring a single rear door and non-standard side panels. The Danish Post Office used these vans for a time.

An indication of the scale of CKD production is provided by this 1950 photograph celebrating the completion of the two-thousandth Morris Minor vehicle at the Motor Assemblies plant in Durban, South Africa.

content, and production climbed steadily. Such was the demand that special dispensation was given for the use of locally designed jigs for body construction and the use of mechanical components including engine, gearbox and back-axle parts manufactured at the Nuffield-backed engine plant based in Sydney. Local content was particularly high in the Australian models, with paint, interior trim materials and electrical parts being sourced from suppliers in Australia. This has resulted in some interesting variations in specification, particularly in the paint and trim combinations offered.

New Zealand also has a distinguished record in the assembly of CKD Morris Minors. Substantial numbers of vehicles, including a high percentage of light commercials, were assembled at the Dominion Motors plant in Auckland. Significantly, production continued here long after it had ceased in the United Kingdom, with vans and pick-ups ('utes') being built until 1974.

On the Indian sub-continent and in South Africa the Morris Minor proved popular mainly because of its durable qualities and its reliability. In South Africa 33,000 vehicles were built at the Motor Assemblies plant in

Durban during the period 1950–64. In India, plants in Calcutta and Madras produced a steady flow of Morris Minors. Production was particularly high in the 1950s, with many saloons being pressed into service as taxis. The longevity of the vehicles and the ingenuity of the local populace was proved many times over as numerous vehicles remained in service decades later. In an interesting marketing ploy the Morris Minor was dubbed the 'Baby Hindusthan' – no doubt in deference to the larger Morris Oxford Series MO, which was sold as the Hindusthan 14.

Smaller-scale assembly and production took place elsewhere, including Mexico, where the Automoviles Ingeleses Company produced Morris 1000 models, and the Philippines, where the Mascott Trading Company assembled saloons and tourers in the early 1950s.

The combined effect of all these overseas operations was to increase substantially the total sales of the Morris Minor worldwide. When these are added to the number of vehicles that were produced in the United Kingdom and exported to important markets such as the United States and Canada, the overall impact was significant. The revenue produced was a welcome boost but, more importantly, the Morris Minor gained a worldwide reputation as being a solidly produced, reliable vehicle. The fact that it has survived in considerable numbers and has such an enthusiastic following by car enthusiasts all over the world is testimony to that.

Assembly plants in Australia and New Zealand were among the most prolific outside the United Kingdom. Many of the CKD vans had side windows fitted.

For people with an
eye for a bargain

The Morris Minor 1000 Traveller...

THE TRAVELLER'S CAR

O NE OF THE most popular variants of the Morris Minor is the ash-framed Traveller model. Ironically, it was the last of the Morris Minors to be introduced and, fittingly, it was also the last to be discontinued. During its eighteen-year production run the Traveller established itself as a versatile multi-purpose vehicle. Over 200,000 were manufactured, and for those that have survived there is a ready market, particularly in the United Kingdom, where enthusiasts are willing to pay premium prices for well-restored or original examples with low mileage.

The origins of the Morris Minor Traveller are intrinsically linked to the development of the much larger Morris Oxford Series MO range of vehicles. Development work on a prototype Morris Oxford Traveller began in 1951. Initial ideas of using a separate chassis on which to mount the rear body were dismissed in favour of using the same floor pan as that used in the saloons, albeit with a few small amendments. On to this base platform an ash-framed structure with overarching roof supports was fixed. On the prototype version, plywood side and rear door panels were fitted, along with an aluminium roof panel, in an attempt to reduce the overall gross weight. However, these were dispensed with in favour of lightweight aluminium panels rear of the cab when the Morris Oxford Series MO Traveller went into production in October 1952. With the main principle of the design process established, and the Morris Oxford vehicles proving successful in service, it was a relatively straightforward progression to create a smaller, more compact version based on the best-selling Morris Minor. It was no great surprise, therefore, when a year later, in October 1953, the Morris Minor wooden-framed 'Traveller' was announced at the Earls Court Motor Show, albeit as the 'Morris Minor Station Wagon'.

The introduction of this new model had a big impact on the assembly methods employed at the Cowley works in Oxford. The wooden frame was assembled at the Coventry bodies branch. Skilled craftsmen put together the ash frame and rear doors, which were then treated and varnished prior to the fitting of individual pre-painted aluminium panels. This included the roof

Opposite:
The Traveller's Car proved to be a versatile vehicle for both private and commercial users. It remains one of the most popular Morris Minors produced.

47

Above:
The Morris Minor Traveller has had many different names ascribed to it over the years. Station Wagon, Traveller's Car, Shooting Brake and Woodie are just a few.

Right:
A durable rubber floor covering and a folding front passenger seat were features of the early Traveller's car. (The Smiths clock in the passenger-side glove box is an after-market accessory.)

Prototype models experimented with plywood rear panels in an ash frame.

section and guttering. The completed assembly was then transported by road to the assembly plant at Cowley.

On arrival at the factory the completed rear sections were placed in a specially constructed loft area above the main feed track. When the matching painted steel cab section arrived on the track below, the already completed

Joint marketing was a reflection of the common parentage of the Morris Oxford MO Traveller and the Morris Minor.

MORRIS

TRAVELLERS

CARS

rear section was lowered from the loft. Immediately the two sections were 'married' together with a ring of bolts and a thick rubber roof seal. The Traveller then proceeded to the assembly shop, where in the early years they were assembled on line number 1 along with vans and pick-ups.

There was uncertainty about what to call the new estate version of the Morris Minor. The American-derived 'Station Wagon' label was dropped fairly quickly in favour of the 'Traveller's Car' This in turn was shortened to the now-familiar 'Traveller' designation. What was not in doubt was the many positive attributes of this new model. The Traveller's Car added a whole new dimension – literally – to the Morris Minor concept, a fact not lost on the advertising department, which for years to come would wax lyrical about the advantages of owning and driving a dual-use vehicle.

From a practical family car with ample room for four or five passengers and their luggage, to a light commercial vehicle with a very usable rear platform when the rear seat was folded and stowed, the vehicle was promoted as being ideal for every occasion. Wide-opening rear doors with an automatic lock check device ensured easy access to the rear of the vehicle, and 33 cubic feet of load space was provided when the rear seats were folded forward. Internal appointments were promoted as fashionable, and certainly the complementary trim schemes added to the modern feel of these new vehicles. Separate front seats with a floor change gearbox on the Minor contrasted with the more spacious bench-type front seat of the Oxford, which utilised a column gearchange.

Contemporary advertising brochures extolled the virtues of the light general purpose Morris Minor and its suitability for the school run, weekends away, business and pleasure travel, including the family holiday.

There was more to these vehicles than just the very useful option of multi-purpose use. The Morris Minor's excellent reputation had been built on its driving and handling characteristics as well as its styling and design. All the positive characteristics noted in previous models were deemed to be present in the Traveller. In particular, the smooth ride offered by torsion-bar independent front suspension and the easy manoeuvrability of the vehicle in confined spaces were highlighted. So too was the 803cc overhead-valve engine, which initially was praised for its power and performance as well as its fuel economy. Costs were a big consideration in promoting the vehicle. The cost-effectiveness of having one vehicle that could be used for both private and business use was seen as a huge advantage and, given the prevalence of commercial travellers and door-to-door salesmen in the 1950s, this was an opportunistic marketing ploy. There was a clear need for a small, economical, yet spacious vehicle with easy access to the rear load area. The Morris Minor Traveller fitted the bill admirably, a fact salesmen were encouraged to promote at every opportunity. They also had some flexibility

The illustration says it all. The spacious interior of the Traveller allowed for a multitude of uses.

51

as options existed in terms of specification for the Traveller models. Standard and Deluxe models were available, though the price differential between them was small. Deluxe models had leather seat facings on the front seats, a heater and a passenger-side sun visor fitted as standard. Externally the only difference was the addition of front overriders. For overseas customers, export models had the benefit of flashing indicators and special options on the type of heater required to cope with local climatic conditions.

RANGE UPDATE

The Traveller models underwent an upgrade in 1954. Specification changes were synchronised with the rest of the range. Externally, the main difference was the change in the front grille panel and the repositioning of the sidelight units to a position directly beneath the front headlamps. Internally, the introduction of a changed dash panel featuring a central speedometer with compact instrumentation and open glove boxes added a fresh dimension to the overall appearance, and provided a more modern feel for the driver.

Prices for the Traveller models remained constant. However, in spite of the upbeat nature of the promotional brochures and general advertising, some veiled criticism was levelled at the Traveller models, in particular in the *Motor* road test for 1955 cars. This in part was linked to the power available from the 803cc engine to transport a vehicle that, when fully laden, could legitimately weigh over a ton. Questions were also beginning to be asked about the gearbox, whose ratios were deemed ill-suited to such a heavy vehicle.

Initial euphoria and advertising hyperbole about the 803cc overhead valve engine was tempered somewhat by experience. The heavier Traveller models needed a little more power than the 30 brake horsepower on offer.

questioned. So too was the lack of adjustment on the driver's seat. Clearly, expectations of comfort, performance and styling were increasing.

In spite of these justifiable criticisms, the Traveller still found many willing buyers. For many, the endearing character of the vehicle, combined with further mechanical improvements, was sufficient for them to part with their money. The Traveller retained its place within a broadening portfolio of BMC models, and this was reflected in the move from individual, model-specific promotional materials to range brochures. To its credit, the Traveller continued to attract admirers. Later models featured a number of small refinements such as steering column locks and alternators. Apart from this, though, the vehicles were essentially the same as those that had entered production in 1964, and people were starting to ask how long the Traveller could retain a significant market share in an increasingly competitive market place.

One way in which this was achieved was to look to fleet orders to boost sales. Lower-specification Traveller models were commissioned for use by the armed forces and other government agencies. Apart from being painted in distinctive colours (military bronze green for the Army, blue grey for the RAF, and black for the Navy), these vehicles had plain-coloured interior trim panels and a one-piece rubber mat for floor covering. In the period 1966–71 some 2,048 vehicles were supplied, and of these 746 were left-hand-drive models for the British Army on the Rhine (BAOR).

Local tax concessions in Denmark resulted in the production of this unique version of the Traveller, which had metal sides in place of the normal window arrangement.

THE FINAL YEARS

DURING the late 1960s Morris Minor sales declined steadily. Few amendments or updates were made to the specifications, and it was generally accepted that although the Morris Minor was a good solid car, it lacked the refinement of some of its more modern contemporaries. In 1968, when Leyland and BMC merged to form British Leyland, annual production had dropped to 31,640 and many of the overseas plants had ceased production. Although many people expected that as a result of the merger Lord Stokes would discontinue production of the Morris Minor immediately, it was not until June 1969 that the first step towards phasing out the Morris Minor was taken, when the last convertible was produced. This was not entirely unexpected, as the open-topped models had not been selling well. In the year of the merger only 346 convertibles had been produced, and by the time production ended only a further 170 had been built.

Competition was fierce within the British motor industry in the late 1960s. Even within the newly formed British Leyland group, the Minor faced stiff opposition from the new Austin Maxi and, more importantly, from the popular Austin/Morris 1100/1300 range. With plans advanced for a new Morris model – the Marina – it seemed only a matter of time before production would finally cease at Cowley. The grim realisation that the profit margin on each Morris Minor produced in 1968 was in single figures, together with diminishing sales, resulted in the production of saloons being discontinued at Cowley on 12 November 1970 in order to make way for the new Morris Marina production lines.

Though this was a significant blow, it did not signal the permanent end to Morris Minor production. Sales of light commercial vehicles were holding up well, no doubt boosted by the decision taken in 1968 to extend badge engineering and market the vans and pick-ups as Austin as well as Morris. In addition, honouring significant contracts, such as those held by the Post Office and British Telecom, and the fact that there was a niche market for the popular Traveller models, combined to make it viable to continue production at the Morris Commercial car plant at Adderley Park, Birmingham.

Opposite:
The last series of Morris Minors (Series 5) featured the 1,098cc version of the reliable A Series engine, improved lighting arrangements front and rear (as shown here), heat-formed vinyl upholstery, and a revised dash panel arrangement.

Right:
Development work
on the final updates
to the Morris Minor
took place on this
prototype four-door
saloon, which was
eventually released
for sale in 1966.

Below:
Late-model Morris
Minor saloons
proved popular with
numerous police
forces when unit
beat policing was
introduced.
Distinctive features
included a Bermuda
blue and white
livery and a zipped
headlining, to
allow access to
the illuminated
police sign.

Production continued until April 1971, when the decision was at last made to end production of the Morris Minor completely in Britain. After twenty-two years and a production run that had seen 1.6 million Morris Minors produced, the end was almost nigh. On the other side of the world, in New Zealand, Minors continued to be made until 1974 at the Dominion Motor Company, though numbers were small.

History had been made. The Morris Minor was the first British car to sell a million, and its principal designer, Alec Issigonis, was knighted in 1969 in recognition of his contribution to the British automotive industry. More importantly, the cars had proved their worth. Many of the innovative design features of the original cars remained throughout the long and prolific production run.

The Series 5 Morris Minors featured the 1,098cc version of the reliable A Series engine.

In the years since production ended many thousands of Morris Minors
have continued to provide sound and reliable transport. Hundreds have been
uprated and updated with larger engines, improved braking and more
comfortable interior fittings. Dedicated owners throughout the world have
ensured the continued use and preservation of these much-loved vehicles,

Left: Interest in preserving and restoring Morris Minors remains high. This rare 1954 van, owned by the author, has been imported from New Zealand and fully restored to its original specification.

Below: The Morris Minor still features prominently in historic saloon car championships.

and as a result a thriving industry has been established to manufacture both mechanical and body parts to assist with restoration, refurbishment and servicing. Body panels are being made in Sri Lanka and imported into Britain. Demand for convertible models has been such that enterprising owners are having two-door saloons converted into open-topped models. Approved kits, with all the necessary additional strengthening pieces, are available to enable the change to be completed in the knowledge that the resulting vehicle is safe to use. Kits are also available to replace the ash frame as fitted to the Traveller models, and new traditional or modern replacement interiors are available from approved heritage suppliers for all models in the range. A thriving worldwide network of clubs ensures that there is a continuing exchange of technical information, as well as a social network for like-minded enthusiasts.

Whether restored to original showroom condition or upgraded for twenty-first-century everyday use, the vehicles retain the charm that has endeared them to millions of owners all over the world. The prospects are good that many thousands of Morris Minors, now cherished as historic vehicles, will survive so that future generations of motorists can appreciate a truly remarkable vehicle that has justifiably acquired iconic status.

Interest remains high in restoring vehicles like this convertible to original showroom condition.

FURTHER READING

Bardsley, Gillian. *Issigonis. The Official Biography*. Icon Books, 2005.
Christianson, Virgil. *The Minor in Miniature*. Privately published, 2003.
Harvey, Russell. *Morris Minor Commercials*. Tempest Publishing, 2000.
Harvey, Russell. *Minor Commercial*. Nostalgia Road Publishing, 2004.
Newell, Ray. *Morris Minor and 1000* (Super Profile Series). Haynes/Foulis, 1982.
Newell, Ray. *Series MM Morris Minor* (Super Profile Series). Haynes/Foulis, 1984.
Newell, Ray. *Original Morris Minor*. Bay View Books, 1992; revised 1995.
Newell, Ray. *Original Morris Minor*. Herridge and Sons Ltd. Reprinted 2007.
Newell, Ray. *Morris Minor – The First Fifty Years*. Bay View Books, 1997.
Newell, Ray. *Morris Minor: The Complete Story*. Crowood Press, 1998.
Newell, Ray. *Morris Minor and 1000 Essential Buyers Guide*. Veloce Publishing, 2007.
Newell, Ray. *Morris Minor: 60 Years on the Road*. Veloce Publishing, 2007.
Practical Classics Traveller Restoration. Kelsey Publishing, 1992.
Pressnell, Jon. *Exploring the Legend*. Haynes, 1998.
Pressnell, Jon. *Morris Minor: The Official Picture Album*. Haynes, 2008.
Robson, Graham. *The Cars of BMC*. Motor Racing Publications, 1987.
Schoenbrunn, Reiner. *The New Zealand Morris Minor*. Transpress New Zealand, 2002.
Skilleter, Paul. *The World's Supreme Small Car*. Osprey, third edition 1989.
Tyler, Jim. *Morris Minor Restoration, Preparation, Maintenance*. Osprey, 1995.
Wainwright, Martin. *Morris Minor: The Biography*. Aurum Press, 2008.
Wood, Jonathan. *Alec Issigonis: The Man who Made the Mini*. Breedon Books, 2005.
Young, Philip. *The Himalayan Minor*. Speedwell Books, 1987.

PLACES TO VISIT

Haynes International Motor Museum, Sparkford, Yeovil, Somerset BA22 7LH.
Telephone: 01963 440804. Website: www.haynesmotormuseum.com
Heritage Motor Centre, Banbury Road, Gaydon, Warwickshire CV35 0BJ.
Telephone: 01926 641199. Website: www.heritage-motor-museum.co.uk
Lakeland Motor Museum, Holker Hall, Cark-in-Cartmel, Grange-over-Sands,
South Lakeland, Cumbria LA11 7PL. Telephone: 01539 558509.
Website: www.lakelandmotormuseum.co.uk
Llangollen Motor Museum, Pentre Felin, Llangollen, Denbighshire, North Wales LL20
8EE. Telephone: 01978 860324. Website: www.llangollenmotormuseum.co.uk
Coventry Transport Museum, Millennium Place, Hales Street, Coventry CV1 1JD.
Telephone: 024 7623 4270. Website: www.transport-museum.com
National Motor Museum, John Montagu Building, Beaulieu, Brockenhurst, Hampshire
SO42 7ZN. Telehpone: 01590 612345. Website: www.beaulieu.co.uk

CLUBS

The Morris Minor Owners Club, PO Box 1098, Derby DE23 8ZX.
Telephone: 01332 291675. Website: www.mmoc.org.uk
The Cornwall Morris Minor 1000 Club, Brian Herbert, 40 Penwethers Lane, Truro, TR1
3PW. Telephone 01872 274815. Website: www.cornwallmorrisminorclub.co.uk

INDEX

Page numbers in italics refer to illustrations